A New True Book

EARTH

By Dennis B. Fradin

CHILDRENS PRESS®

CHICAGO

Most of the Earth's surface
is covered by water.

AP/Wide World Photos—41 (right)

Cameramann International Ltd.—17 (left, top & bottom right), 37, 44 (top left), 45 (bottom right)

Historical Pictures Service, Chicago—19

NASA—13, 14, 25 (left)

© Rob Outlaw—12 (right), 16 (top right)

Photri—9, 10, 16 (center right), 25 (right), 36 (2 photos), 40 (left), 43 (right); © R. Harding, 45 (left)

R/C Photo Agency—© Richard L. Capps, 44 (top right)

Root Resources—© Kenneth Rapalee, 41 (left)

Tom Stack & Associates—© Larry Brock, 7; © Don & Pat Valenti, 12 (left); © Tom Stack, 15; © Thomas Kitchin, 16 (left), 43 (left), 44 (bottom right); © Spencer Swanger, 16 (bottom right); © Dave Mlllert, 32; © John Gerlach, 35; © John Cancalosi, 40 (right); © Ken W. Davis, 42 (left)

Tony Stone Worldwide—Cover; © Richard Passmore, 2; © Doug Armand, 4; © James P. Rowan, 17 (center right); © Roger Mear, 33; © Brad Iverson, 42 (right); © Peter Pearson, 44 (bottom left); © Ben Edwards, 45 (top right)

Illustration—Len W. Meents, 21, 27; John Forsberg, 22; Albert R. Magnus, 28, 31, 39

Cover — Earth as seen from our moon, © Tony Stone Worldwide

For My Friends, John and Sue Wirman

Library of Congress Cataloging-in-Publication Data

Fradin, Dennis B.
  Earth / by Dennis B. Fradin
    p.   cm. — (A new true book)
  Includes index.
  Summary: Discusses the Earth as a planet and describes its temperatures, movements in space, and other characteristics.
    ISBN 0-516-01172-3
    1. Earth—Juvenile literature.
[1. Earth.] I. Title.
QB631.4.F73   1989   89-9982
525—dc20   CIP
                                       AC

TABLE OF CONTENTS

OUR SUN, THE STAR

On a clear night, our eyes can see about 2,000 stars in the sky. Stars are huge balls of hot, glowing gas. People who study stars and other heavenly bodies are called astronomers. By using telescopes, astronomers have learned that there are many, many millions of stars.

Of all those stars, just one appears in the daytime. It is a yellow star we call the Sun.

The Sun is not special when compared to other stars. Its size is just average. Its brightness is just average. And its heat is just average for a star.

Why does the Sun seem so big, bright, and hot to us? The reason is that the Sun is by far the closest star to Earth. The Sun gives off the heat and light we need to live. Without it, there would be no life on our planet Earth. There wouldn't even be an Earth.

The Sun is the center of our Solar System.

THE SUN'S FAMILY, THE SOLAR SYSTEM

Stars cannot be home to living things. They are much too hot. The Sun is about 10,000° F at its surface. Blue-white stars are five times as hot.

Living things can exist on planets, though. Planets are large objects that move around stars. We are living proof that life can exist on planets!

Probably many stars besides the Sun have planets. But we know the most about the Sun's nine planets. We call these Mercury, Venus, Earth, Mars, Jupiter, Saturn, Uranus, Neptune, and Pluto. Most of

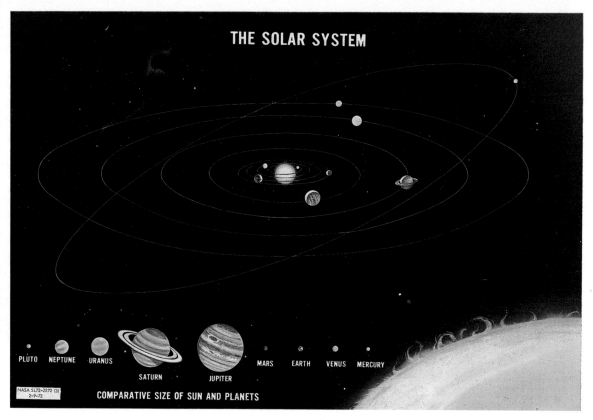

THE SOLAR SYSTEM

PLUTO NEPTUNE URANUS   MARS   EARTH   VENUS   MERCURY
              SATURN   JUPITER

NASA SL72-2272 (3)
2-9-72   COMPARATIVE SIZE OF SUN AND PLANETS

the planets have moons that
move around them.

The Sun, planets, and
moons are the main bodies
in the Solar System. The
Solar System can be thought
of as the Sun's "family."

9

People live and grow food on the part of the
Earth's surface that is covered by soil.

The other eight planets
can only be seen in the sky.
But you don't have to look at
the sky to see our planet
Earth. Just look down at the
ground! In fact, the name
"Earth" comes from old words
10 that refer to the ground.

EARTH IS JUST RIGHT FOR LIFE

The eight planets besides Earth do not seem to have any advanced forms of life. Some planets are too hot for plants and animals. Some are too cold. And none of the other eight has the air and the water that plants and animals need.

People enjoy the wonders of Earth.

Luckily, though, one of the Sun's planets is "just right" for life. It is neither too hot nor too cold. It has air to breathe and water to drink. That planet is our wonderful Earth!

SHOULD IT BE CALLED "PLANET OCEAN"?

From space, Earth looks like a blue and white ball. The blue is water. About 70 percent of our planet is

Astronauts aboard the *Apollo* spacecraft took this photograph of Earth.

Can you find the continent of North America
under the clouds?

covered by water. Nearly all
of that is ocean water. So
much of Earth is covered by
oceans that some people
say it should have been
called Planet Ocean!

Some of the white patches

are ice and snow on the ground. Some are clouds in the sky.

About 30 percent of Earth is land. Earth's largest landmasses are called continents. Smaller pieces of land surrounded by water are called islands. The land often looks yellowish-green from space.

Islands off the coast of Norway

Earth's land has great variety. In places, tall masses of rock and dirt rise out of the ground. These are called mountains. Earth's tallest peak, Mount Everest, rises about

5½ miles above sea level. Earth also has large stretches of dry areas called deserts, and wet, steamy tropical rain forests. In cold regions it has huge ice masses called glaciers.

EARTH IS ALWAYS MOVING

All the stars and everything else in space make up the universe. Long ago, people thought that Earth stood still. They thought the stars and other heavenly bodies circled Earth.

For thousands of years, people believed the Earth stood still. Then the famous Polish astronomer Nicolaus Copernicus proved that this

Copernicus was the first astronomer to prove that the Earth travels around the Sun.

idea was wrong. He said that heavenly bodies seem to move across the sky because Earth spins. People slowly realized that Copernicus was right.

Today, we know that our Earth moves in four main ways.

19

1) *Earth spins.* Earth is always spinning. It takes about 24 hours to rotate (spin) once. As we spin, it appears to us that the Sun, Moon, planets and stars are moving across the sky.

Earth's spinning causes day and night. As your part of Earth spins into view of the Sun, the Sun seems to rise for you. You have day. Meanwhile, the Sun is out of view for people on Earth's other side. They are having

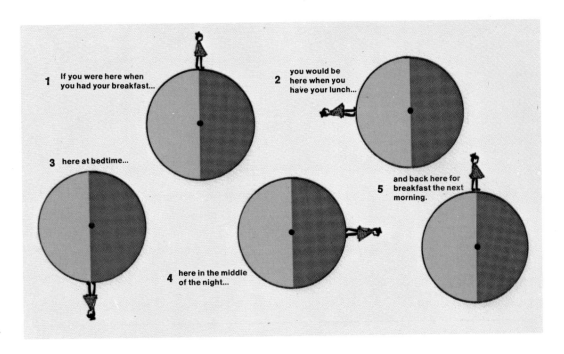

1 If you were here when you had your breakfast...

2 you would be here when you have your lunch...

3 here at bedtime...

5 and back here for breakfast the next morning.

4 here in the middle of the night...

night. When your part of Earth spins away from the Sun, you have night. But people on the other side of Earth are enjoying their daytime.

2) *Earth orbits the Sun.* Besides spinning, Earth also moves around the Sun in an

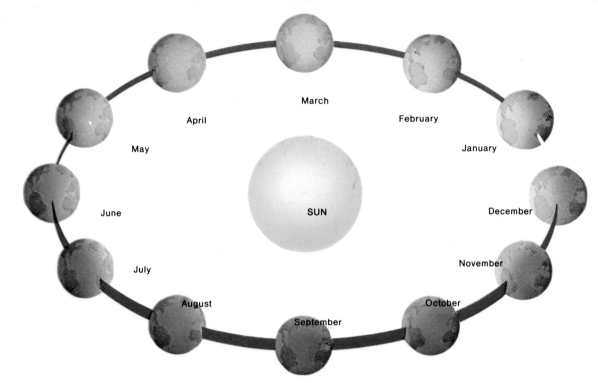

As the Earth rotates, it moves around the Sun.

egg-shaped orbit. It takes
about 365¼ days for Earth
to orbit the Sun. That is the
length of one year.

Earth's movement around
the Sun causes the seasons.
At different times of the year,

the Sun shines from different angles on any spot on Earth. When it shines directly on Earth's northern half, that region has summer. But meanwhile, the Sun is shining from a lower angle on Earth's southern half. That region is having winter. Six months later, things switch around. Earth's southern half has summer. The northern half has winter.

Earth orbits the Sun at about 67,000 miles per hour.

Count to 5. In that time Earth has moved about 100 miles in its yearly orbit around the Sun!

3 and 4) *Earth moves two ways with the Milky Way galaxy.* The stars are not just scattered across the universe. They are bunched in very large groups called galaxies. The Solar System is part of the Milky Way galaxy. The Milky Way has about 200 billion stars.

The whole Milky Way—

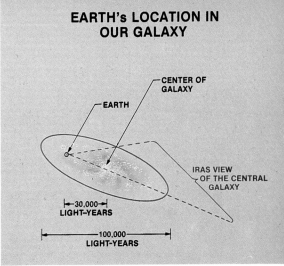

CENTER OF GALAXY

EARTH

IRAS VIEW OF THE CENTRAL GALAXY

30,000
LIGHT-YEARS

100,000
LIGHT-YEARS

Earth and all the other planets are part of the Milky Way galaxy. Distances in space are so huge they are measured in light-years. A light-year is the distance at which light travels in one year. One light-year is equal to 5,878,000,000,000 miles.

including the Solar System— is revolving like a pinwheel. It is revolving at 150 miles per second. Not only that, the whole Milky Way is moving through space at 400 miles per second.

If Earth is moving four ways, why can't we see or feel it? When we throw a ball in the air, why isn't it left behind by the moving Earth? Why aren't we spun off the planet?

There are several reasons. For one thing, the air moves along with Earth. Also, Earth is very big and moves very smoothly. And Earth has a force called gravity that holds things down to it.

EARTH'S SIZE, INSIDES, AND TEMPERATURES

MERCURY

VENUS

EARTH

MARS

Earth is the only planet in the Solar System where we could live. But in size Earth is just average. It is bigger than Pluto (the smallest planet), Mercury, Mars, and

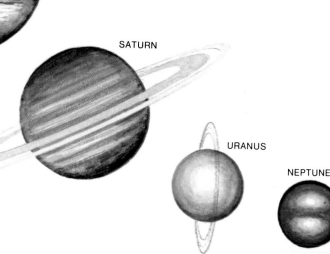
JUPITER

SATURN

URANUS

NEPTUNE

PLUTO

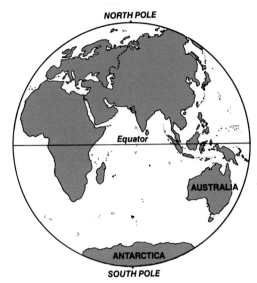

The equator is an imaginary line around the center of the Earth. The Northern Hemisphere is north of the equator, and the Southern Hemisphere is south.

Venus. It is smaller than Jupiter, Saturn, Uranus, and Neptune. Earth could fit inside Jupiter, the biggest planet, about 1,400 times.

The equator is an imaginary line that circles Earth's middle. Earth is about 24,900 miles around at its equator. Pretend you are in a vehicle that can go 60 miles an hour over land or water. At that rate, it would take about 17 days to circle Earth at the equator.

There is a joke about a child who visits a beach for the first time. "The ocean sure has lots of water!" says the child. "That's nothing," says the parent. "You're just looking at the top of the ocean. Think how much water there is underneath!" The same thing is true of

Earth. We see just its outside surface. Earth goes down very deep to regions we can't see. By studying rocks and earthquakes, scientists have learned about Earth's insides.

Earth has three main layers. They are the crust, the mantle, and the core.

We live on top of the crust, which is a little like an egg's shell. The crust goes down about twenty miles beneath land. It goes down about

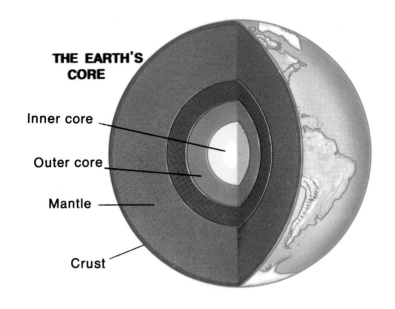

THE EARTH'S CORE

Inner core

Outer core

Mantle

Crust

three miles beneath the
ocean.

Below the crust is a thick
layer of hot rock called the
mantle. The mantle goes
down about 2,000 miles. The
hottest rock in the mantle
reaches a temperature
of about 4,000° F.

Hot molten lava flows from a volcano in Hawaii.

The core is the very hot center of our planet Earth. Scientists think the core is made of metals—some solid and some melted. The core's hottest part may reach nearly 10,000° F. That is about the temperature of the Sun's surface!

Ice cliffs on Barne Glacier in Antarctica

Things are much cooler on top of the crust, where we live. Earth's average surface temperature is a little under 60° F. The hottest recorded temperature was 136° F, in Libya. The coldest recorded temperature was -127° F, around the South Pole.

33

EARTH'S MOON

All of the nine planets except Mercury and Venus have moons orbiting them. Saturn has the most—over twenty moons. Earth has just one moon, which we call the Moon.

The Moon is big—for a moon. In fact, it is a little larger than the planet Pluto. But the Moon is much smaller than Earth. About fifty Moons could fit inside our planet.

The reason the Moon
looks so big in the sky is that
it is so close to us. The Moon
is about 240,000 miles from
Earth. It is Earth's nearest
neighbor in space. Our next-
nearest neighbor, Venus, is
over one hundred times as
far away as the Moon.

Astronauts explored the surface of the moon in 1969.

The Moon is the only
heavenly body that people
have visited. United States
astronauts first landed on
the Moon on July 20, 1969.
They had to wear space
suits on the Moon. The Moon
has no air or water. It is as

hot as an oven in some places. It is colder than a freezer in other places.

You would weigh less on the Moon than you weigh on Earth. If you weigh 72 pounds on Earth, you would weigh 12 pounds on the Moon. Because of its smaller size, the Moon has less gravity to hold things down.

OUR EARTH'S PAST AND FUTURE

Scientists have learned Earth's age by studying rocks. Earth is about 4.5 billion years old. It was probably formed at the same time as the rest of the Solar System.

The Solar System may have begun as a cloud of dust and gas. Parts of this huge cloud shrank. The central part may have fallen into the Sun. Other parts may have become the planets and their moons.

For most of its past, Earth has been different than it is now. At first it may have lacked air, water, and life. Later it may have had one big continent instead of the seven it now has. During the

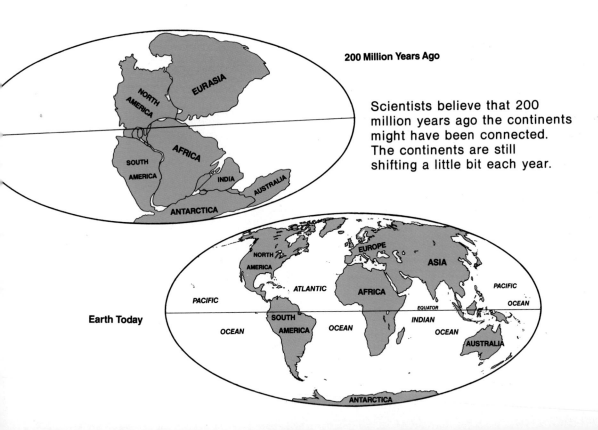

200 Million Years Ago

Scientists believe that 200 million years ago the continents might have been connected. The continents are still shifting a little bit each year.

Earth Today

Ice Ages, Earth was colder than it is now. At other times, it was warmer than today.

Various life forms have come and gone on our planet. Millions of years ago, dinosaurs ruled the Earth. Then they all died. About two million years ago, people

Dinosaurs, such as the Stegosaurus (left) and the Parasaurolophus (right), once lived on Earth.

Museum exhibit (left) recreates the world of *Homo erectus*. From a skull found in Africa by Dr. L. S. B. Leakey, an artist drew the face of Zinjanthropus (right) who might have lived on Earth 1,750,000 years ago.

first appeared. That is like a blink of an eye in Earth's history.

Our Earth should last another three billion years— the time the Sun has left to shine. If people exist when the Sun dies, they may be able to find another planet to call home. But will people still be here even a few thousand years from now?

Humans have spoiled Earth by allowing poisonous chemicals and dangerous waste materials to pollute our air and water.

The problem is that we have dirtied Earth's air, water, and land. In other words, we have polluted our planet. If we don't take

better care of Earth, we could go the way of the dinosaurs. For the sake of future people, shouldn't we do a better job of caring for our beautiful planet Earth?

FACTS ABOUT EARTH

Average Distance from Sun— 93 million miles

*Diameter—*7,927 miles

*Length of Day—*About 24 hours

*Length of Year—*About 365¼ days

*Average Temperature on Surface—*About 57° F

*Atmosphere—*Nitrogen, oxygen, argon, and tiny amounts of other gases

Highest Point on Land— Mount Everest, 29,028 feet above sea level

*Lowest Point on Land—*Along the Dead Sea, about 1,310 feet below sea level

*Average Speed as Earth Orbits the Sun—*About 18.5 miles per second

WORDS YOU SHOULD KNOW

astronomer(ast • RAH • nih • mer)—a person who studies stars, planets, and other heavenly bodies

billion(BILL • yun)—a thousand million (1,000,000,000)

continents(KAHN • tih • nents)—Earth's largest landmasses

core(KOHR)—the very hot center of Earth

crust(KRUHST)—the top level of Earth

Earth(ERTH)—the planet (the third from the Sun) on which we live

equator(ih • KWAY • ter)—an imaginary line that circles Earth's middle

galaxy(GAL • ex • ee)—a group of millions of stars moving together in space

gravity(GRAV • ih • tee)—the force that holds things down to a heavenly body

mantle(MAN • til)—a thick layer of hot rock beneath Earth's crust

Milky Way galaxy(MIL • kee WAY GAL • ex • ee)—the galaxy in which we live

million(MILL • yun) — a thousand thousand (1,000,000)

moon(MOON) — a natural object that orbits a planet; Earth has one moon, which we call the Moon

orbit(OR • bit) — the path an object takes when it moves around another object

planet(PLAN • it) — a large object that orbits a star; the Sun has nine planets

pollution(puh • LOO • shun) — the dirtying of Earth's air, water, and land

rotate(ROH • tait) — to spin

Solar System(SO • ler SISS • tim) — the Sun and its "family" of objects

star(STAHR) — a giant ball of hot, glowing gas

Sun(SUHN) — the yellow star that is the closest star to Earth

telescope(TEL • ih • skohp) — an instrument that makes distant objects look closer

universe(YOO • nih • verss) — all of space and everything in it

INDEX

About the Author

Dennis Fradin attended Northwestern University on a partial creative scholarship and was graduated in 1967. His previous books include the Young People's Stories of Our States series for Childrens Press, and Bad Luck Tony for Prentice-Hall. In the True book series Dennis has written about astronomy, farming, comets, archaeology, movies, space colonies, the space lab, explorers, and pioneers. He is married and the father of three children.